# SPOTLIGHT ON NATURE
# POLAR BEAR

MELISSA GISH

CREATIVE EDUCATION / CREATIVE PAPERBACKS

Published by Creative Education and Creative Paperbacks
P.O. Box 227, Mankato, Minnesota 56002
Creative Education and Creative Paperbacks are imprints
of The Creative Company
www.thecreativecompany.us

Design by Chelsey Luther; production by Joe Kahnke
Art direction by Rita Marshall
Printed in the United States of America

Photographs by Alamy (Arterra Picture Library, Vlad Ghiea, imageBRO-
KER, National Geographic Image Collection, Nature Picture Library),
Buffalo Zoo, Dreamstime (Isselee, Johnypan), iStockphoto (4FR, JHaviv),
Minden Pictures (Ingo Arndt/NPL, Alberto Ghizzi Panizza, Dave Watts/
Nature Production), National Geographic Creative (DESIGN PICS INC,
RALPH LEE HOPKINS, KEITH LADZINSKI, ROBERT HARDING PIC-
TURE LIBRARY, NORBERT ROSING, KONRAD WOTHE/MINDEN
PICTURES), Shutterstock (Hung Chung Chih, FloridaStock, Eric Isselee,
Anastasiia Malinich)

Library of Congress Cataloging-in-Publication Data
Names: Gish, Melissa, author.
Title: Polar bear / Melissa Gish.
Series: Spotlight on nature.
Includes index.
Summary: A detailed chronology of developmental milestones drives this life
study of polar bears, including their habitats, physical features, and conserva-
tion measures taken to protect these clear-haired marine mammals.
Identifiers: LCCN 2019060154 / ISBN 978-1-64026-343-7 (hardcover) /
ISBN 978-1-62832-875-2 (pbk) / ISBN 978-1-64000-485-6 (eBook)
Subjects: LCSH: Polar bear—Juvenile literature. / Habitat conservation—
Juvenile literature.
Classification: LCC QL737.C27 G58 2020 / DDC 599.786—dc23

First Edition HC 9 8 7 6 5 4 3 2 1
First Edition PBK 9 8 7 6 5 4 3 2 1

# CONTENTS

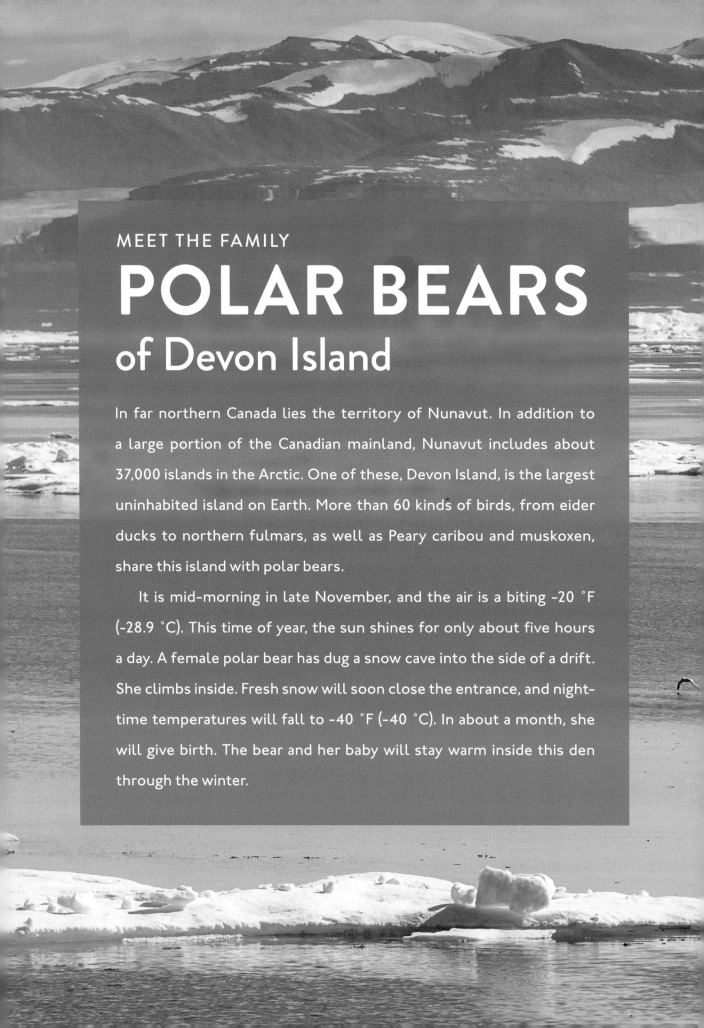

MEET THE FAMILY

# POLAR BEARS
## of Devon Island

In far northern Canada lies the territory of Nunavut. In addition to a large portion of the Canadian mainland, Nunavut includes about 37,000 islands in the Arctic. One of these, Devon Island, is the largest uninhabited island on Earth. More than 60 kinds of birds, from eider ducks to northern fulmars, as well as Peary caribou and muskoxen, share this island with polar bears.

It is mid-morning in late November, and the air is a biting -20 °F (-28.9 °C). This time of year, the sun shines for only about five hours a day. A female polar bear has dug a snow cave into the side of a drift. She climbs inside. Fresh snow will soon close the entrance, and night-time temperatures will fall to -40 °F (-40 °C). In about a month, she will give birth. The bear and her baby will stay warm inside this den through the winter.

# Eyes

A nictitating (*NIK-tih-tay-ting*) membrane protects polar bear eyes from snow blindness. This see-through eyelid closes to shield the eyes from water and blowing snow.

# CHAPTER ONE

# LIFE BEGINS

The polar bear is one of eight bear species and the only one suited to life in harsh Arctic regions. All bears are mammals, meaning they are warm-blooded, typically give birth to live young, and produce milk to feed their offspring. As marine mammals, polar bears depend on the ocean to survive. Their main food sources—beluga whales, seals, nar-whals, and walruses—live in the sea. Polar bears walk over the frozen ocean, or sea ice, and swim from place to place—sometimes traveling for days without stopping.

Of the world's roughly 25,000 polar bears, at least 15,000 inhab-it the Canadian Arctic. The rest are found in Alaska, Greenland, Rus-sia, and Svalbard. Most polar bears remain active year round, unlike

DEVON ISLAND POLAR BEAR MILESTONES

**DAY ①**

- Born
- Ears and eyes closed
- Sparse fur, none on ears
- Weight: 1 pound (454 kg)
- Length: 12 inches (30.5 cm)

other bear species, which enter a deep sleep called hibernation during winter. Only pregnant females bury themselves in a snow den for four or five months while their babies, called cubs, develop. Although their body systems slow down (they do not eat, drink, or produce waste), mother polar bears remain awake to care for their helpless young. During storms, polar bears may dig impressions in the snow and curl up with their paws over their faces. Snow then covers them like a blanket, protecting them from the wind.

## CLOSE-UP
# Sniffing out food

Polar bears can smell a carcass 20 miles (32.2 km) away. The scent of seawater, which carries from more than half a mile (0.8 km) away, indicates breaks in the ice where they can grab prey.

## FEATURED FAMILY

# Welcome to the World

An icy wind blows across Devon Island. The mother polar bear is cozy and warm inside her maternity den. With little effort, she gives birth to a tiny female cub. The cub's eyes are closed, and her ears are folded back. Her short fur is sparse compared with her mother's. The mother gently pulls the cub close and licks her clean. The cub grunts softly as she snuggles into the warmth of her mother's fur.

POLAR BEAR
825 POUNDS

BROWN BEAR
560 POUNDS

SPECTACLED BEAR
230 POUNDS

GIANT PANDA
215 POUNDS

From a birth weight of about one pound (454 g), polar bears grow to be one of the largest predators on Earth. Fully grown males, called boars, average about 1,000 pounds (454 kg) but can be 1,700 pounds (771 kg) where food is abundant. Standing on their hind legs, boars can be up to 11 feet (3.4 m) tall. Females, called sows, are half the weight of males and usually stand about seven feet (2.1 m) tall.

④ **WEEKS**

- Eyes open
- Weight: 5.5 pounds (2.5 kg)

Though polar bears appear white, their fur is actually transparent. It looks white because it reflects light. To survive in their cold habitat, polar bears have about one million hairs per square inch (6.5 sq cm). Long, hollow guard hairs keep water away from the skin. Dense underfur holds heat close to the bear's body. Beneath their black skin is a layer of insulating fat up to four inches (10.2 cm) thick.

— FEATURED FAMILY —

## First Meal

The polar bear cub was born with tiny claws, but she cannot yet grip and must rely on her mother to hold her close for warmth. The cub's sense of smell draws her to one of the four nipples on her mother's chest. The rich milk her mother produces will help the cub grow quickly. Feeding every few hours, she will gain more than 20 pounds (9.1 kg) by the time her mother leads her out of the snow den and introduces her to solid food in springtime.

To survive in their **COLD** habitat, polar bears have about

ONE MILLION

hairs per square inch (6.5 sq cm).

(7) **WEEKS**

▸ Milk teeth erupt
▸ Takes first steps
▸ Vision is clear

Polar bears have 21 pairs of teeth, including 2 pairs of 2-inch-long (5.1 cm) canines. Cubs' first teeth erupt after about seven weeks. Permanent teeth replace them when cubs are five to six months old.

# CHAPTER TWO

# EARLY ADVENTURES

Polar bear cubs are about four weeks old when their eyes open. In another three to four weeks, they can see clearly, and their milk teeth begin to erupt. By 10 weeks of age, cubs are crawling around the den and climbing on their mother. If a sow gave birth to two or three cubs, the siblings play together. The mother keeps the den clean by eating her cubs' waste. When cubs are about four months old, the mother digs out of the den. By this time, cubs weigh between 22 and 33 pounds (10–15 kg) and have sharp teeth. The family remains near the den for about 10 days so that cubs can become accustomed to the cold air and practice walking on snow.

Since a mother polar bear goes without eating while inside the den, she loses weight. She must find food soon after emerging in

## (10) WEEKS

- Plays and climbs on mother
- Coat is thicker, with fully furred ears
- Weight: 13 pounds (5.9 kg)
- Length: 20 inches (50.8 cm)

**CLOSE-UP**
## Seal hunting
A polar bear's torpedo-shaped head and long neck are ideal for hunting seals. The bear patiently waits by a breathing hole. When a seal surfaces, the bear launches itself headfirst into the hole, grabbing the seal in its jaws.

FEATURED  FAMILY

# Look Who's Learning

The polar bear cub is now eight months old. Drinking her mother's milk and sharing the meat that her mother catches have helped her reach a weight of 99 pounds (44.9 kg). The cub is watching her mother at the water's edge. She is already learning that food appears at breaks in the ice. Young seals are splashing about, unaware of the danger nearby. Suddenly, the mother and daughter spot another polar bear coming toward the water. The cub lets out a startled cry. Her mother lowers her head and rushes forward, telling the stranger to back off. The bear turns away. The cub relaxes and turns her attention back to the hunting lesson.

When **cubs** are about

# 4 MONTHS OLD,

the mother digs out of the den.

 **MONTHS**

- Leaves den for the first time
- Rides on mother's back in water
- Weight: 26 pounds (11.8 kg)

# Give It a Try

This is the young polar bear's first winter on the ice. As a yearling, she still relies on her mother for both milk and prey. Right now, she smells what her mother smells: food. A young walrus has become separated from its family and swims alone amidst broken pieces of ice. Following her mother, the polar bear cub jumps into the frigid sea. The walrus is an easy catch. Together, the cub and her mother haul their meal out of the water.

**CLOSE-UP**
# Paws and claws

Twelve-inch-wide (30.5 cm) paws act like snowshoes, keeping the bear on top of snow and ice. The footpads' fleshy bumps and tiny indentations, plus fur between the pads, give traction. Curved four-inch-long (10.2 cm) claws snag and hold prey.

order to remain strong enough to care for her offspring. Cubs follow their mother to the sea, where ice breaks up in the spring. Their fur is not yet waterproof, and they do not have enough insulation to keep them warm in the icy water, so they avoid getting wet. If their mother is forced to swim to find food, they ride on her back. When a mother polar bear captures a seal or other prey, she rips off the skin to reach the blubber beneath. Her young cubs join in, getting their first taste of solid food.

**(6) MONTHS**

- Swims for the first time
- Permanent teeth replace milk teeth
- Begins to share mother's meals

**(8) MONTHS**

- Uses teeth to peel sealskin
- Weight: 99 pounds (44.9 kg)

# Diving and swimming

Polar bears can dive to 15 feet (4.6 m) and hold their breath for about 2 minutes. Their nostrils pinch shut underwater. Partially webbed front paws act as paddles. Polar bears can swim about 6 miles (9.7 km) per hour nonstop for more than 60 miles (96.6 km).

# CHAPTER THREE

# LIFE LESSONS

Polar bears spend about two and a half years with their mothers. During this time, cubs learn and practice skills they will need to survive on their own. Mothers teach cubs how to ride out storms by curling up and placing their paws over their muzzle. Cubs learn to walk with their head down to sniff for prey. They figure out which scents mean food and which mean danger. Mothers fiercely defend their offspring from predators, but only one out of three polar bear cubs survives to age two. A juvenile bear's worst enemy is an adult male polar bear. If attacked, there is simply no defense against the bigger, stronger bear. Wolf packs can also pose threats, but if the young bear can reach water, the wolves will not follow.

Polar bears can live to be 25 years old. Females are fully grown by

## (14) MONTHS

- Learns to find breathing holes by scent
- Weight: 160 pounds (72.6 kg)
- Height: 3.7 feet (1.1 m)

## (24) MONTHS

- Eats only solid foods
- Weight: 363 pounds (165 kg)
- Height: 5 feet (1.5 m)

five or six years old. They usually mate for the first time at this age and continue to have cubs every three or four years. Males do not reach full size or seek mates until they are 8 to 10 years old. To find each other during mating season (and to avoid each other the rest of the year), polar bears leave scent marks with their paws. During mating season, males track down females whose scent indicates a readiness to mate.

Male polar bears may travel hundreds of miles to find mates. At first, a male and female are cautious of one another. Since males are so much bigger than females, this meeting can be dangerous. Males have been known to kill and eat females if they are terribly hungry. If a

— FEATURED FAMILY —

# This Is How It's Done

At 30 months old, the polar bear is now a juvenile. She paws at a bird nest on the ground. Her mother, preparing to mate again, has walked away for the last time. Suddenly, a wolf pack appears. The young polar bear groans loudly. Her mother turns, but she's too far away to help. She can only watch her youngster run. The wolves rocket forward. The juvenile is no match for these predators on land. As the wolves close in, the bear leaps into the sea. She's safe—for now.

<table>
<tr><td>（30）MONTHS</td><td>（5）YEARS</td></tr>
</table>

**30 MONTHS**

- ▸ Separates from mother
- ▸ Survives wolf attack
- ▸ Catches a seal every 5 or 6 days

**5 YEARS**

- ▸ Fully grown
- ▸ Weight: 910 pounds (413 kg)
- ▸ Height: 7 feet (2.1 m)

female senses that she cannot trust a male, she will try to run away. But if the female trusts the male, they will spend about a week building a relationship. They hunt together and share meals. They sleep curled up together. After mating, they go their separate ways to continue their solitary lives on the snow and ice.

## CLOSE-UP
# Keeping clean

Dirty fur reduces insulation. After feeding for about 30 minutes, a polar bear dips its paws and face in water or rolls in the snow to wash. It will do this several times as it eats. Afterward, it will spend extra time washing.

FEATURED FAMILY

# Practice Makes Perfect

Caribou graze on summer vegetation that pokes through the permafrost. Most of the new calves stick close to the herd, but one has wandered away from its mother. Though blubber is her preferred food source, the young polar bear will not give up any chance for a meal. Her mother prepared her well. She charges forward and lunges at the baby caribou, instantly killing it with a bite to the head. After her feast, the leftovers will feed neighboring Arctic foxes and rough-legged hawks.

|  **6** YEARS | **21** YEARS | **23** YEARS |
|---|---|---|
| ▸ Digs maternity den<br>▸ Gives birth for the first time | ▸ Injures paw guarding prey from rival<br>▸ Hunting skills decline | ▸ End of life |

# CHAPTER FOUR

# POLAR BEAR SPOTTING

In the early 20th century, polar bears were hunted for their fur and body parts. By the 1960s and '70s, as their numbers declined, hunting was strictly limited or completely banned. In Canada, Greenland, the United States, and parts of Russia, only native peoples (such as the Aleut, Inuit, and Yupik) can legally hunt polar bears today. Poaching is the illegal killing of animals. This is a problem for polar bears in many places, including Russia's Chukotka (Chukchi) Peninsula. About 200 polar bears are poached there every year.

While some polar bear populations are stable, others have declined by as much as 30 percent since 1990. This is mostly because of climate change. Polar bears rely on frozen seas to hunt. Arctic sea ice used to remain frozen almost the whole year. Now, rising global temperatures cause more than 70 percent of sea ice to melt each summer. It forms later in winter and breaks up earlier in spring. This shortens winter, when polar bears feed and fatten up before the summer thaw. Survival is especially difficult for pregnant females who must live off their stored fat while buried in snow dens with new cubs.

Longer, hotter summers may soon leave nothing but open ocean, forcing polar bears to swim great distances to find prey. They are excellent swimmers, but without sea ice, they may tire and drown. Many simply starve. Polar bears forced inland in search of food are drawn to garbage. These bears are often killed to prevent conflict with humans. As polar bears change their natural behaviors in attempts to survive, scientists work to protect polar bears and humans from each other. Some communities use remote cameras to provide early warning of approaching polar bears. Wildlife managers can then redirect polar bears away from settlements.

In 2017, a team led by the U.S. Fish and Wildlife Service published a plan to protect polar bears. It states that the best thing humans can do for polar bears is to find ways to help them adapt to their changing environment and minimize our impact on them. This means providing protection for denning mothers, further limiting hunting, and protecting Arctic waters from pollution and oil spills. Above all, the report states, we must curb climate change. Humans can help polar bears survive if we take the threat of climate change seriously.

# SNAPSHOTS

The closest **polar bear** relative is the **brown bear**. Brown bears can be found in dense forests, high plains, and open tundras across North America, Europe, and Asia.

The tropical **sun bear** is nicknamed "honey bear" for its love of honey. Its four-inch-long (10.2 cm) claws easily tear open beehives.

Every October, tourists visit Churchill, Manitoba, on the shore of Hudson Bay. Hundreds of **polar bears** gather there ahead of the coming freeze.

The **spectacled bear** is the only living bear species native to South America. Males are twice as big as females.

A close **polar bear** cousin, the **Himalayan brown bear** is named for its mountain home. This bear hibernates from October to April.

The **sloth bear** of India, Nepal, and Sri Lanka feeds on fruit, ants, and termites. Its long muzzle and nimble lips work like a vacuum to suck up insects.

Grizzly bears are a **brown bear** subspecies found in the interior forests of Canada and the U.S. They are smaller than **polar bears**.

The **giant panda** is found only in China. Fewer than 2,000 of these rare bears exist in the wild.

The **Asian black bear**, which ranges from northeastern Russia to Malaysia, is also called the moon bear. The white mark on its black chest looks like a crescent moon.

About 3,000 **polar bears** live on Svalbard, an island group in the Arctic Ocean belonging to Norway.

The **Kodiak bear** is a **brown bear** subspecies found only on Alaska's Kodiak Archipelago. It is about the same size as the **polar bear**.

**"Pizzly"** is a common nickname for the offspring of a **grizzly** and a **polar bear**. This hybrid was first discovered in 2006.

The **American black bear**, found throughout North America, is more closely related to **Asian black bears** than to **polar bears**.

# WORDS to Know

**blubber**  the thick layer of fat between skin and muscle of marine mammals

**carcass**  the body of a dead animal

**hybrid**  the offspring of two plants or animals of different species or varieties

**insulating**  protecting from the loss of heat

**permafrost**  an upper layer of permanently frozen soil

**snow blindness**  a temporary blinding caused by light reflecting off white snow

**species**  a group of living beings with shared characteristics and the ability to reproduce with one another

# LEARN MORE

## Books

Borgert-Spaniol, Megan. *Polar Bears*. Minneapolis: Checkerboard Library, 2019.

Castaldo, Nancy F., and Karen de Seve. *Mission: Polar Bear Rescue: All About Polar Bears and How to Save Them*. Washington, D.C.: National Geographic Society, 2014.

Roome, Hugh. *Polar Bears*. New York: Children's Press, 2018.

## Websites

"Polar Bear." National Geographic. https://www.nationalgeographic.com /animals/mammals/p/polar-bear/.

"Polar Bear." San Diego Zoo Animals & Plants. https://animals.sandiegozoo .org/animals/polar-bear.

"Polar Bears." Polar Bears International. https://polarbearsinternational.org /polar-bears.

## Documentaries

Clarke Powell, Nick. *The Great Polar Bear Feast*. Renegade Pictures, 2015.

Pontecorvo, Joseph. "Bears of the Last Frontier: Arctic Wanderers." *Nature*, season 29, episode 16. Rubin Tarrant Productions, 2011.

Ravetch, Adam, and Sarah Robertson. *Polar Bears: Ice Bear*. Arcadia/Arctic Bear Productions, 2013.

Note: Every effort has been made to ensure that any websites listed above were active at the time of publication. However, because of the nature of the Internet, it is impossible to guarantee that these sites will remain active indefinitely or that their contents will not be altered.

# Visit

## AKOOK ARCTIC ADVENTURES

*Boats take visitors around barrier islands to observe polar bears in their native habitat.*

838 8th Street

Kaktovik, AK 99747

## COLUMBUS ZOO AND AQUARIUM

*Thanks to the zoo's breeding program, polar bear cubs are periodically exhibited.*

4850 West Powell Road

Powell, OH 43065

## DETROIT ZOO

*Visitors can watch polar bears swim overhead in the Polar Passage.*

8450 West 10 Mile Road

Royal Oak, MI 48067

## MARYLAND ZOO

*This zoo conducts research and promotes conservation in partnership with Polar Bears International.*

One Safari Place

Baltimore, MD 21217

# INDEX